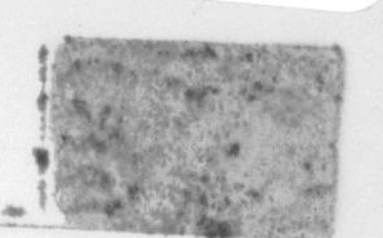

THE INCA

Also by the same author

THE APACHE INDIANS
Raiders of the Southwest

THE CHEROKEE
Indians of the Mountains

THE CHIPPEWA INDIANS
Rice Gatherers of the Great Lakes

THE CROW INDIANS
Hunters of the Northern Plains

THE DELAWARE INDIANS
Eastern Fishermen and Farmers

THE ESKIMO
Arctic Hunters and Trappers

HORSEMEN OF THE WESTERN PLATEAUS
The Nez Perce Indians

INDIANS OF THE LONGHOUSE
The Story of the Iroquois

THE MISSION INDIANS OF CALIFORNIA

THE NAVAJO
Herders, Weavers, and Silversmiths

THE PUEBLO INDIANS
Farmers of the Rio Grande

THE SEA HUNTERS
Indians of the Northwest Coast

THE SEMINOLE INDIANS

THE INCA

INDIANS OF THE ANDES

By SONIA BLEEKER

Illustrated by Patricia Boodell

WILLIAM MORROW & COMPANY

New York 1960

Published simultaneously in the Dominion of
Canada by George J. McLeod Limited, Toronto.
Printed in the United States of America.

Library of Congress Catalog Card Number: 60-5179

CONTENTS

THE INCA

I

INCA CONQUESTS

The Inca Empire—the Empire of the Sun—flourished in the Andean highlands on the west coast of South America between 1438 and 1533—a brief but meteoric hundred years. The Inca Indians conquered this rough, mountainous region in a series of wars against other Indian tribes. By 1533 the Inca Empire extended over the entire stretch of mountain ranges, the Cordilleras (Cor-dee-yer′-ahs), in what is now Ecuador, Peru, and northern Chile, and included a chunk of southwest Bolivia and northern Argentina as well.

The land along the Pacific coast is mostly barren, near-desert country, with hardly any life on it during the dry spells. In some places in northern Peru it never rains, or rains only once in seven years. Because of the dryness, large quantities of fertilizer are preserved on the offshore islands—the famous guano islands. From the coast the land rises abruptly eastward and forms plateaus which are some 20,000 feet high. The Cordilleras reach heights of 22,000 feet.

The Andean highlands are cut by rivers flowing east and west. The rivers which flow westward toward the Pacific are short, steep, and turbulent. The rivers flowing toward the eastern jungles of the Amazon region are longer. These eastward-flowing rivers form the headwaters and drainage of the Amazon River.

Except for the desert stretches and the formidable snow-covered mountain peaks, the rest of the country, severe as it is, was inhabited in Inca times, as it is today. Its people had lived there for many, many centuries. They must have originally come from North America, through the

Inca Empire 1438–1533 A.D.

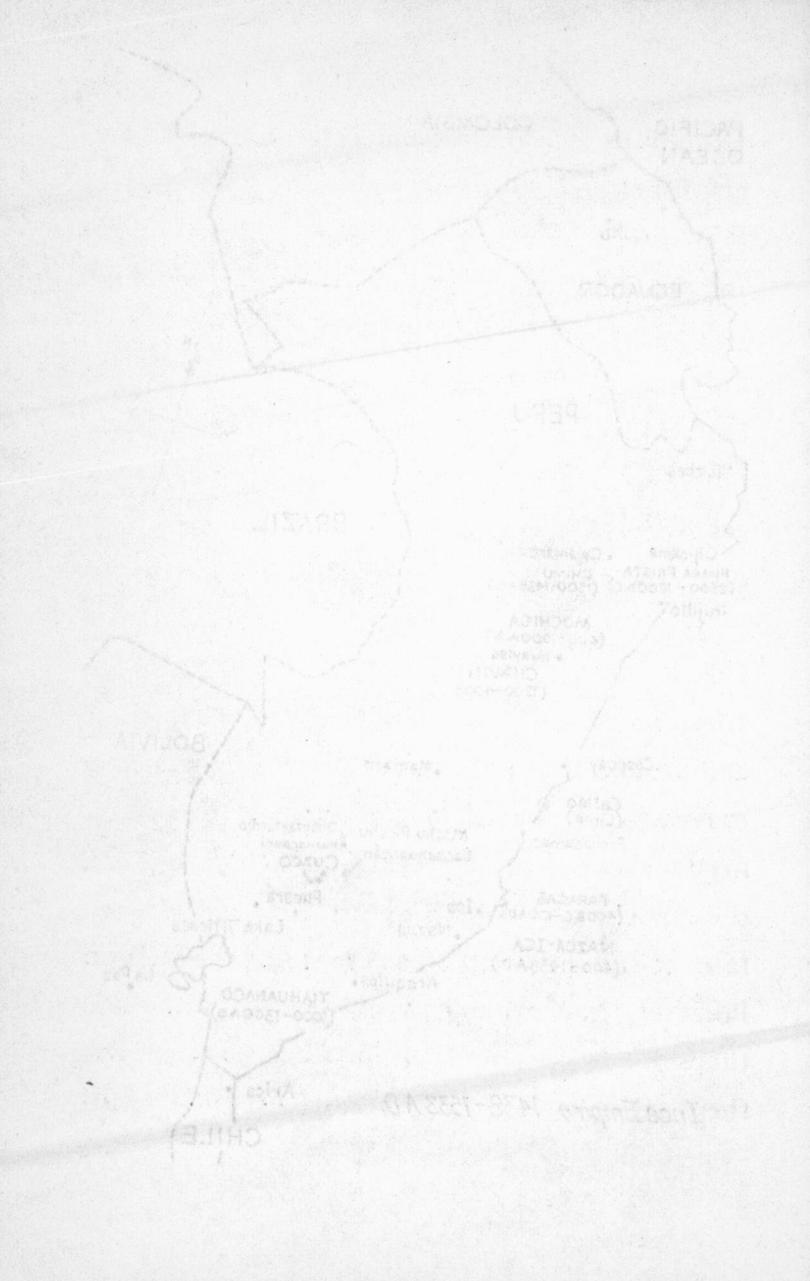

Isthmus of Panama—wandering groups of hunters, fishermen, and plant gatherers.

Most Peruvians do not like the heat of the jungles. They prefer the cool highlands, the high valleys formed by the east-flowing rivers. There are five of these basins in the Andean highlands: Cajamarca, Callejón de Huaylas, Mantaro, Cuzco, and Titicaca. These were the main centers of life during the time of the Inca Empire, and they are still the main centers today.

The Inca Empire originated in the region of Cuzco Basin, sometime around 1200 B.C. The Inca maintained that they had always lived in and around that area. Usually, if a people have moved from one region to another, they have myths about their migrations. The Navajo and the Apache of North America, for example, tell tales of coming down from the north. The Inca, however, had no myths about migration, and therefore we assume that the Cuzco region was their native land as far back as they could recall —perhaps 5000 years.

The basic unit of Inca society was the ayllu (eye′-you), a group of people related to a common ancestor. The body of the ancestor was wrapped in layers and layers of cotton cloth, and his descendants—his sons and grandsons—prayed to him. The men in an ayllu owned land in common; they farmed together, helping one another with the planting, sowing, and harvesting; and they gathered together on feast days to worship their common ancestor. To this day the Andean Indians like to work together and help one another, and the ayllu is still a very important family and social unit.

We do not know why one ayllu among the Inca began to be looked upon as royal; perhaps its men were more ambitious and more numerous. We do know, however, that the Inca had thirteen great rulers from the beginning of their Empire until 1533, and that the founder of the first royal ayllu was Manco Capac. His body was not preserved, because he was, according to legend, of supernatural origin, and he turned to stone when he died.

LAKE TITICACA

There are two legends about the beginnings of the Manco Capac ayllu. One says that Manco Capac and his family of three brothers and four sisters came out of a cave in the southeast of Cuzco. According to the other version, Manco Capac and his sister, Mama Ojllo (Oh′-yo), were children of the Sun and were sent down by the Sun to an island in Lake Titicaca. After searching for a suitable place to live, they founded the town of Cuzco, which became the capital of the Inca dynasty. They taught the people they found around Cuzco to raise corn and to weave cloth. Their first son, Sinchi Roca, began the conquest of Peru.

Legends have it that under the first three rulers who came after Sinchi Roca, Inca rule was extended to Lake Titicaca, to Tiahuanaco—which was then a very important town—to the headwaters of the coastal rivers, and to some of the coastal fishing villages. The next three rulers continued the expansion of the Empire.

In the early days of the Inca, conquest and

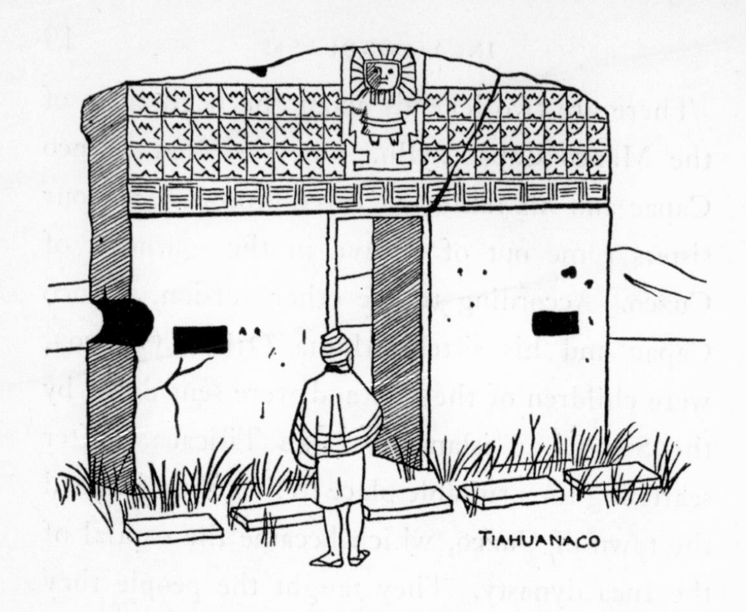

expansion were not accomplished by means of huge armies. Probably the small Manco Capac ayllu allied with a neighboring Inca ayllu and moved against still another neighbor. After conquering them, the Inca let the people remain on their land and allowed the craftsmen to continue their pottery making, weaving, and metalwork. Inca soldiers returned at each harvest to collect an annual tribute of corn and llamas. The pottery, weaving, and metalwork of some of these conquered people were superior to those of the

Inca, but the Inca were ready to learn from them.

As the might of the Inca increased, they began to take advantage of each warring group outside their borders. Weaker nations often asked their help against a strong enemy aggressor, and in exchange for this help, the Inca received tribute in produce from both the weaker nation and the newly conquered aggressor.

There were always struggles for power within the royal house—Manco Capac had found it necessary to kill his three brothers—and there were threats from the outside, too. As the territory under Inca control grew larger, the danger of rebellion among the conquered peoples increased. Therefore, they were no longer permitted to live as they had before the conquest, merely paying tribute in men and produce. The Inca often issued orders to kill all the men in a newly conquered village, and to escape this fate the defeated men fled to the mountains or into the jungle immediately after battle.

Pachacuti Inca Yupanqui, the ninth ruler of

the Inca, is the first emperor for whose reign we have exact dates. By his time (1438 to 1471) the Inca Empire was well established. To insure obedience to himself, Pachacuti ordered all the people of Cajamarca, a newly conquered province in the northern highlands, to move south. He moved to Cajamarca people who had been living longer under Inca rule and could be trusted not to rebel. This was the beginning of enforced mass migrations. Any village that seemed rebellious or refused to turn over the produce tax imposed by the Inca was resettled elsewhere in the Empire. This was not done without a struggle, since the farmers loved their homes and their land. But the Inca won, and rebels were moved away from their relatives and friends and made to live among strangers. Indians do not trust strangers, whose ways and language are unfamiliar to them, and Pachacuti knew that people who were suspicious of each other would not plan revolt together.

Pachacuti's son, Topa Inca, continued the northward and southward conquests. By the end of his reign, in 1493, the Empire had spread into northern Ecuador and central Chile, covering an area of some 350,000 square miles. The Inca and their allies numbered among the people they had conquered many, many tribes, with as many different languages. These tribes, due both to the Inca conquest and the later Spanish enslavement, have long since lost their identity and language. We no longer know even their names, and their ancient history is forgotten, too.

The little of the Andes that remained to be conquered by the Inca was won by Huayna Capac, who ruled from 1493 to 1525. He conquered the area around the Gulf of Guayaquil and returned to Cuzco with tribute in emeralds, mother-of-pearl, and turquoise. He continued his conquests southward and brought back gold, silver, and bronze from Bolivia.

Like other emperors, Huayna Capac had many wives and children. To avoid strife between Atahuallpa and Huascar, who were his eldest sons by two different wives, Huayna divided his kingdom between them. Atahuallpa ruled from Cajamarca, while his brother Huascar ruled from Cuzco. But Atahuallpa was not happy with his share of the kingdom, and he had his brother killed. Atahuallpa became the sole ruler of the Inca Empire at almost the same time as the Spaniards arrived.

Historians say that two runners reached Atahuallpa almost simultaneously. The one from Cuzco brought word that Huascar had been killed. The messenger from Tumbes, on the coast, reported that the boats of the Spanish had been sighted and that they were debarking. "They are bearded men," the runner said, "with large, fat animals, like short-necked llamas."

By 1532, when the Spaniards arrived, the Inca had developed one of the three great civilizations in South America. Their system of government, which was built up like a pyramid, was remarkably well organized. At the very top of the pyramid was the emperor, and at the base were the farmers and craftsmen. In each village there were overseers who were responsible for the welfare of ten families. They kept track of the marriages, births, and deaths in these families. Over them were the *curacas*, lesser members of the nobility, who were responsible for 100 families. People came to the overseers with their problems and grievances, and, in turn, the overseers got advice from the *curacas* on problems they themselves could not solve.

The *curacas* worked under a nobleman who was responsible for 500 families. Together with him they sat in court, listened to complaints, and administered justice. The law was strict. When a man confessed to an error, he was forgiven by the Inca gods, but not by the judges. They set a death penalty for him and his family.

The next group in the pyramid were nobles who were responsible for 1000 families each. There were also nobles responsible for 10,000 families and for 40,000 families. Finally, there were four wise men of royal blood, who were responsible directly to the emperor for the entire population. For greater convenience the Inca had divided the Empire into four slices, and each of these men presided over a province. The Northwest was called *Chinchasuyu;* the Southwest, *Cuntisuyu;* the Northeast, *Antisuyu;* and the Southeast, *Collasuyu.* The Inca called their Empire *Tahuantinsuyu*—the Land of the Four Quarters.

The population of the Land of the Four Quarters was between eight and sixteen million. It included thriving, hard-working farmers, outstanding potters, weavers of fine textiles, craftsmen who worked in gold and silver, and builders of huge stone temples that stagger the imagination even today. Quechua (Kech′-wah), the language of the Inca, was the dominating language of this Empire, and Inca culture had put its stamp on everything.

2

THE INCA HIGHWAY

The Inca conquests could never have been accomplished without good roads, nor could the Inca have continued to rule over the conquered peoples for long without being able to move armies to any troubled part of the Empire with lightning speed.

The great Inca Highway, which ran from north to south, is still being discovered by our archeologists. It was actually two almost parallel highways, paved with cobblestones, with many crossroads connecting them. One highway stretched along the entire Pacific coast from the town of Tumbes in northern Peru to Talca in Chile. This highway serviced the coastal villages and towns. Numerous roads connected these settlements with the main road.

The other highway, which was even more traveled, ran inland from Quito, Ecuador, to Cuzco, the capital of the Inca Empire. South from Cuzco the highway forked, circling Lake Titicaca and continuing south through Bolivia to the town of Tucumán in Argentina. From Tucumán the highway turned west to the port of Coquimbo in Chile. From Coquimbo a highway led to what is now Santiago, and still another highway led from Tucumán to Mendoza in Argentina. In all, the Inca Highway covered over 2000 miles, a distance comparable to the entire length of the Atlantic coast from Maine to Key West, Florida.

To have built roads in this land of lofty mountains and high plateaus, deep gorges, scraped-out canyons and turbulent rivers, was quite a feat. The Inca's ingenuity in overcoming these obstacles was amazing. In some places, where the grade was too steep for a loaded man or llama, wide stone steps were built to make the climbing easier. Wherever possible, the Inca dug tunnels. Raised causeways were laid out over narrow passes between peaks or over shallow bodies of water. Canyons and rivers were spanned with bridges.

One of these bridges, which was built—it is believed—in 1350, served the highland people for hundreds of years before it collapsed. This bridge was the subject of a book by Thornton Wilder, entitled *The Bridge of San Luis Rey*. The bridge, according to Mr. Wilder, was 250 feet long. It hung over the gorge of the turbulent Apurimac River, some 90 feet below. The Andean people called the Apurimac River the Great Speaker, because its rushing waters, echoing and re-echoing in its deep gorge, were never silent. The bridge was built of braided and twisted fibers, held together with matting and mud. Two thick plaited fiber rails were needed to steady the traveler, because the bridge swung in the air with the wind.

The Inca Highway took years and years to

build. Men from each family unit in every village and town along the way were drafted for the work. Crews with overseers kept all the roads open and in good repair. They constantly reinforced weak stretches of highway with terraces and stone walls, and they added improvements all the time. These men were exceptional stonemasons, and they always did their best, no matter how small the job. They even decorated the stone walls with designs to please the travelers.

Although the Inca did not encourage the common people to travel, there were always Indians on the highway. They traveled by day, and at night they slept on mats on the side of the road, with only their blankets to protect them against the bitter cold of the highland nights.

On market days the highway was crowded with people. The Inca government accumulated surplus grain in its warehouses, and annually distributed it to the people. If a family had enough grain of their own, they could take it on market day and trade it for cloth, pottery, or ornaments.

Craftsmen turned out small articles of wood, which they exchanged for pieces of llama hide or some produce their family needed. Good potters, both men and women, traded their wares for the gourds that other Indians raised. Highland women traded llama and alpaca wool for cotton grown in the valleys, and the fishermen in the coastal towns dried their catch and carried it in baskets to the highlanders. A family with a few extra ducks carried them alive to market to exchange for cloth or fish, sandals, or a copper pin.

When ducks were brought to market, the woman of the household did the trading, and her husband went with her to make sure that she was well treated. Since the ducks really belonged to the little daughter, who, with her mother's help, had raised them, fed them, and watched over them, she came along to watch the trading and learn how it was done. The son went to market too, to watch and to learn. And so, at dawn, entire families set out along the village paths and made their way to the highway.

The Inca administrators attempted to restrict the movements of the common people by allowing them only three market days a month, but trading went on all the time, because the people enjoyed it. Always there was an exchange of artifacts; and people, carrying bundles, went back and forth along the highway.

An Indian man placed his bundle in a sack and tied the ends of the sack across his chest. Heavier bundles were supported by a band across the forehead. A woman wore a shawl, fastened in front with a pin, and wrapped her bundle inside it. She

sometimes slipped the shawl over her head when she did not want to be stared at. Both men and women used the walking time to spin thread. The men, huddled inside their wool capes, kept a steady pace despite worn sandals and rough, wet stone pavements. A woman walked behind her husband, her spindle twirling, her baby secure on her back. The child, lulled to sleep by the rhythm of his mother's walking, was no trouble at all. When he asked for food, the mother either nursed him or fed him some corncake, which she carried in a bag slung across her chest.

Although llamas and alpacas were seen on the highway, no one rode them—not even small children. These animals, natives of the Peruvian highlands, carry smaller loads than a man does. They are not as hardy as burros, donkeys, or

camels, although llamas, like camels, can get along without water for a long time. Llamas can travel only about fifteen miles a day in the high altitudes of 12,000 to 16,000 feet. Sure-footed, they follow their leader over the steepest trails,

but when they get tired, they simply sit down and refuse to budge. If a llama is urged or whipped, it will turn its long neck and spit at the driver. At the day's end, llamas are led out to graze in the highland meadows, where they feed contentedly on the tough ichu grass, which is so dry that all other animals refuse to eat it.

The common people walked along the highway, but the nobility were carried in litters. The floor of a litter was made of boards, which rested on two long poles. The poles, in turn, rested on the shoulders of four men. The litters were enclosed by curtains, and inside there were low stools on which the travelers sat. The litters of the emperor's household glittered with gold and jewels, and were sometimes preceded and followed by a retinue of a few thousand warriors, armed and ready for combat.

The sight of Inca warriors marching down the highway must have been dazzling. Although the soldiers averaged no more than five feet, three inches in height, their headdresses, painted with geometric figures and topped with shiny decorations of hammered copper, added at least eight inches to their height. The few hairs they had on their faces were plucked out with tweezers. They wore their straight hair long. The face of the Inca soldier—with its high cheekbones, arched nose, and low forehead—was painted with heavy black, red, and yellow stripes. Each soldier carried a shield made of boards covered with skins and decorated with cloth or feathers. De-

spite their simple weapons—clubs, spears, slings, shields, and a sharp knife for hand-to-hand combat—the Inca soldiers awed their enemies with their fierce appearance.

Along the highway, every four to eight miles, were small stations called *tampus*. Inside them were places where noblemen could spent the night. Next to the *tampus* were storage rooms where an army could quickly get any additional food it needed. Most important of all, however, was the use of *tampus* in the Inca's messenger system.

The Inca's system of runners, or *chasquis*, was remarkable. Messengers ran day and night along the highway. They were given right of way by the other travelers. Two runners were always stationed at a *tampu*, and they kept constant watch for messengers. When a runner was sighted, the watchman sprinted out of the *tampu* and continued running with the new arrival, who did not lessen his pace. As they ran, the tired messenger turned over the bundle or message he was carrying to the fresh runner. The fresh runner continued on;

the tired runner turned back to the *tampu* to eat, sleep, and await his turn to make the return journey.

Men trained to become runners for the govern-

ment. This job was part of the village *mita*—the labor each man had to give to the community. A man worked as a runner for some fifteen days and then returned home to his family, his farming, and other household activities—till his next turn came.

Relay runners could carry a message across the length of the Empire from Cuzco to Quito—a distance of over twelve hundred miles—in five days. The Inca boasted that within three days after a fisherman caught a fish at the port of Callao, near Lima on the Pacific coast, the fish would be cooked by one of the emperor's wives and served up, still fresh, on a gold platter on the emperor's table at Cuzco. This was not an idle boast, for the Inca's amazing system of roads had made such rapid travel possible. The Inca Highway was one of the greatest achievements of the Inca Empire, an achievement that road builders and engineers still marvel at today.

3

THE INCA AT HOME

The ways of the land and of men change very slowly. Watching the people in a Peruvian highland village today, you can see many faces that resemble those carved in ancient stone and molded in clay. In the towns there are many people of Spanish descent and still more who are cholos—a mixture of Indian and Spanish—but in the villages the majority of the people are still Indian. They make up more than sixty per cent of the population.

The Inca Indian, like the average Peruvian farmer today, did not want to leave his village.

He came to town to trade, to attend festivals, and to see the sights, but he regarded the town as a noisy, hustling place and was always glad to get back to the familiar, to the quiet and peace of his village.

The size of a village usually depended on its location. High up in the mountains, where the land was poor and rocky, a family or two might live alone in their huts, in the midst of their fields. Sometimes a village was built up in two sections, with fields in the center and a few homes at either end. In the valleys, however, where the land was more fertile and able to support a greater number of farmers, the villages were larger.

A man chose as the site for his home a place where something good or fortunate had happened to him. The Inca called such a place a huaca (wah′-kah). Perhaps a mountain ridge or a ledge of a particular shape inspired a feeling of awe and so became huaca to him.

Nothing was too small or too steep to build a hut on, provided that water was nearby or could be brought in artificially in a man-made aqueduct. In time the area around the house was leveled and built up with boulders to make a terrace. This provided room for another hut, which would house a newly married son or brother. Since farming land was so precious, the sites for the huts were usually on barren, steep ground which was unsuitable for farming. As a village grew, people crowded their huts together until the village became a jumble of houses, corrals, pens, and patios. Paths between houses were very narrow—just wide enough for a man and his burden or a llama with a pack on its back.

When a hut crumbled with age, the owner's heirs built another hut atop the old foundations, and after several generations a village tended to rise many feet above its original site. Archeologists find the remains of generations of householders in these abandoned village sites: pottery fragments (sherds), pieces of leather and cloth, old toys, stone tools, knives, animal bones, corncobs, gourds, and human burials. Skillfully interpreted, these become a history book for the archeologist to read, and, in turn, to interpret to us. Thus we are able to learn something of the lives of these people, who had no written history.

The home of an Inca farmer was a square, single-room hut. Together with a few of his relatives and friends, the farmer gathered stones for the foundation of his home. He grooved and fitted them into place. The walls of the hut were built of adobe brick. The men worked together to make the brick, usually making enough to build more than one hut. They dug up the clay dirt, poured water into it, and mixed it with a spade, adding dry grass that had been chopped up into very small pieces. Next they carried loads of the clay to a flat place and pressed it into wooden frames. The frames were the size of the bricks they wanted—about eight inches wide, thirty-two inches long, and three to four inches thick. The men removed the frames and let the bricks dry in the sun for about a week. When they laid the bricks they used long strings with pebbles tied to them as plumb lines, so the walls would be straight and even. The adobe used by the coastal Indians had more sand in it, and their bricks were more square in shape.

The roof was supported by five thin poles, one at each corner and one in the center. It was made of thatch and covered with pebbles and mud to keep the thatch in place.

There were no windows or smoke holes in the hut. The only opening was the doorway, which faced east, toward the rising sun. Most doorways were covered with a blanket or a piece of hide. Wood was sometimes used for doors, but not very often, because most of the trees had been cut down centuries before. The Inca government, in an effort to conserve the few wooded areas that still remained, did not allow anyone to chop down a tree without special permission.

In those high altitudes it is hot during the day when the sun shines. As soon as the sun sets, however, it grows bitterly cold. Men and boys stripped to the waist as they worked outdoors in the sun,

but at the end of the day the people hastened to close their doors tight. At night they slept on grass mats, which rested directly on the mud-packed floor, and covered themselves with animal skins and wool capes to keep warm.

There was no stove or fire inside the hut. It was customary to have a cooking shed, separate from the living quarters, which two, three, or even four neighbors shared. The stove the Indians used was something like a camp stove. It was small, round, and made of clay, with three openings at the top for cooking. Since a meal was usually made in one pot, three women could cook their meals on the stove at the same time. Dried llama dung and grass were used for the fire, which was built through an opening in the side of the stove. This convenient, economical clay stove seems to have been an Andean invention.

The farmer's wife rose before dawn to grind corn for the morning meal. Huddling in her woolen shawl, she ran the short distance from her house to the cooking hut. There she put some llama dung into the side opening of the little clay stove and blew on the embers from last night's fire to start a new fire going.

On one of the burners she set a pot of water to boil. While it heated, she ground dry corn on a large, three-legged, sloping slab of stone. On the stone the woman threw corn kernels, a handful at a time, and with a rocking motion she pressed the kernels with a large handstone, crushing them into flour. She poured the flour into the pot of boiling water, added some peppers, and let the mixture boil into a mush.

When the food was ready, the woman carried the hot pot back into the hut. The family hunched over the meal and ate it quickly. The Indians believed in witchcraft, and they were afraid that a witch might get to their food and sicken them, so they tried to eat it as fast as possible. Often, when a man was among strangers, he ate his food facing a wall, to hide himself from anything evil.

There were only two meals a day, and they varied little from day to day. The Indians ate either corn meal, other cereals and beans, or a simple stew of potatoes and beans. After a harvest, corn was sometimes boiled in its husk. A few times a month, on festive occasions, the Indians ate duck, guinea pig, or, occasionally, the meat of an old llama or alpaca. Whatever meat was left over was pounded and dried carefully in the sun.

A family did not have many possessions. The housewife needed only a few simple cooking utensils for the meals she cooked—some blackened pots, a clay plate or two, and clay spoons. She used the large gourds or clay pots she had made to store her water, corn, beans, dried potatoes, and peppers.

The hut had no furniture. Everyone sat on mats on the earth floor. As the thatching of the roof dried, it shed dust and bits of dried vegetation into the room, so the house was never completely clean and free of dust. Bits of thatching were forever getting lodged in the Indians' clothing and in their long hair.

With so few articles of housekeeping, the Indian hut was almost bare. The walls had wooden pegs in them, on which the family hung any clothing they took off at night. Niches built into the walls served as shelves for household goods, tools, yarn, spindles, musical instruments, toys, and neatly folded festive clothing.

Outside the hut were pens and corrals for llamas and alpacas, a few ducks, and guinea pigs. These animals were the responsibility of the housewife and the children who were too young to work in the fields. Because space was so precious, related households used the same corral for their few animals and shared the small pens.

The Indians lived and worked outdoors most of the time. During the day it was pleasant and warm outside. The woman of the house sat on a mat working on her simple loom, spinning wool, or combing the wool for spinning. She boiled vegetable dyes in a pot in the cooking shed, soaked the wool in a large pot beside her, then washed it and laid it out to dry in the sun.

An Indian woman made all the family's clothing. She wove the long, narrow piece of cotton cloth that her husband used as a breechcloth. The cotton came from the coast, where it was grown in the warm valleys, and the Indians who lived in the mountains traded their wool yarn for it. The woman also wove her husband's long sleeveless shirt, a square piece of cloth with a slit in the center. It reached to his knees, and the sides were either tied with cords or sewed together. She used the wool of an alpaca and a llama to weave the shirt in stripes of brown and black. If she was weaving a shirt for festive occasions, she might mix the black with some white wool, to make a shirt of gray and brown stripes.

The woman also wove the wrap-around skirt or kilt her husband wore over his breechcloth. Her husband's cape had to be long and warm. Since she could not weave a wide piece of cloth on her narrow loom, she wove several strips and sewed them carefully together. A well-made cape lasted a lifetime. Her husband wore it and used it as a blanket at night. When he needed an additional bag to carry produce home from the field, he scooped the ends of the cape together and it served as a basket.

The peaked wool caps with ear flaps, which men and boys wore outdoors, were woven of colored thread and decorated with tassels. A woven or plaited cotton band kept the men's long hair in place. Everyone had a shoulder bag or two, since there were no pockets in the clothing. These were also woven.

Until a boy reached fourteen or fifteen, he wore only a knee-length shirt and a hairband, both modeled after his father's. Girls wore the same garments their mothers wore. These were very simple—a loose, long dress that left the arms bare, and a capelike shawl held together in front by a copper pin.

A housewife on the coast wove her family's clothing of cotton with some wool added. The coast men also wore breechcloths, kilts, shirts, and hairbands, but they did not need capes or wool caps to keep warm.

The Indians always went barefoot at home. Away from home they wore sandals—heavy pieces of llama hide cut to the shape of the foot. Thongs of bast fiber or leather, tied at the heel, over the instep, and between the toes, held the sandals in place.

Like all weavers, the Indian women tried their best to make the clothing not only durable but attractive. Each village had its own styles and weaving designs. People could tell where a man and his family came from by looking at the style of their clothing.

In addition to cooking and making clothes for the family, the Indian housewife had the job of repairing cracks in the walls of her house and replacing the thatching on the roof. Adobe did not last very long in this land of bitter winds and rain and extreme daily changes in temperature, so repairs went on endlessly. Anything that was too hard for the woman to do was done by her husband when he came home.

The life of the wife of a *curaca*—who was responsible for 100 farming families—was not as full of toil as that of a farmer's wife. A *curaca's* home, which was built of stone, was sturdier, roomier, and better situated than a farmer's hut, and *mita* labor kept it in better condition. The interior of the house, however, was almost as simple as the farmer's. There were mats on the floor, and sometimes there were low platforms for beds. A three-legged clay oven burned during the cold nights, so the sleeping family was comfortable and warm. The house had neither windows nor a chimney, but it had a good solid door that shut out the night's cold.

The *curaca's* wife did not have to get up at dawn in a freezing room and rush to grind corn for the morning meal. There were women to help her with the grinding, cooking, and serving. She had a stove all to herself too, and she did not have to share her cooking shed with anyone. Servants tended the plants, the herbs, and the fruit trees in the courtyard garden. Men worked the *curaca's* field and helped to herd the livestock. There was more food in the *curaca's* household, and the two daily meals, which regularly included meat, were more ample and varied.

The *curaca's* family also owned more than one change of clothing. His wife spent many hours at the loom, but she had women helping her with the spinning and weaving. The clothing her family wore was more carefully made, and she used finer wool—sometimes the wool of the vicuña—for the festive clothes.

In the days of the Inca vicuñas ran wild in the highlands of Ecuador, Peru, Chile, Bolivia, and the tropics. Their coat, tawny brown in color with

a white or orange bib, was not thick, but their wool was of the finest quality. The Inca were forbidden to kill vicuñas. Villages organized hunts for vicuñas, however, and sheared them and then released them.

The higher nobility lived in towns. There were many towns in Inca times, towns in the valleys and towns in the highlands. In a typical town the temple was in the center of a spacious plaza. But all roads leading to the plaza were very narrow—just wide enough for a litter and carriers. Homes and government buildings presented solid walls to the street, as they still do in many parts of Central and South America today. Behind the walls were patios or courtyards with gardens and flowers.

A woman of the higher nobility lived in greater comfort than the wife of a *curaca* did, but even the noblewomen worked at their looms, weaving and embroidering the finest and laciest textiles. They wove capes trimmed with the colorful feathers of tropical birds. They worked gold and silver threads into the garments, giving them a beautiful sheen. They also prepared food for their families with the help of servants.

The household of the Inca emperor was, indeed, a show place, as befitted the son of a god. The palace buildings were large one-room dwellings facing spacious patios. The walls were made of stone, skillfully laid by the best craftsmen and stonemasons of the Empire. The palace buildings did not have furniture, but the floors were covered with soft mats and rugs, and the interior walls were decorated with hangings. Some of these hangings were ornamented with hammered gold and silver designs, which depicted the sun, the moon, and the stars, and with birds, llamas, and serpents, which the Inca considered sacred.

Since the emperor had many wives and many, many children, his household was very large—a town in itself. It included numerous servants: craftsmen, silversmiths, pottery makers, and weavers; priests, philosophers, and poets. The priests gave the emperor advice, and the philosophers and poets taught and entertained him.

The emperor saw very few people outside of these wise men and his own family. He was too sacred a person to be seen by the common people. When a nobleman was given the great honor of entering the emperor's chambers, he first had to remove his sandals and tie a heavy burden on his back. Thus barefoot and burdened, even the highest noble appeared humble before the son of the Sun.

The emperor ate his meals alone, served by one of his wives. The wives also prepared his food, each one taking her turn and cooking foods the emperor especially liked. Delicacies were carried in by runners from afar—fruits from the tropics, fish from the coast.

No one dared touch any of the food left over on the emperor's plate. It was destroyed, because it was too sacred to be eaten by a human being, even by one of royal blood. Even the dishes he ate from, it was said, were burned on certain festive days as an offering to the Sun.

It was also said that the emperor never wore the

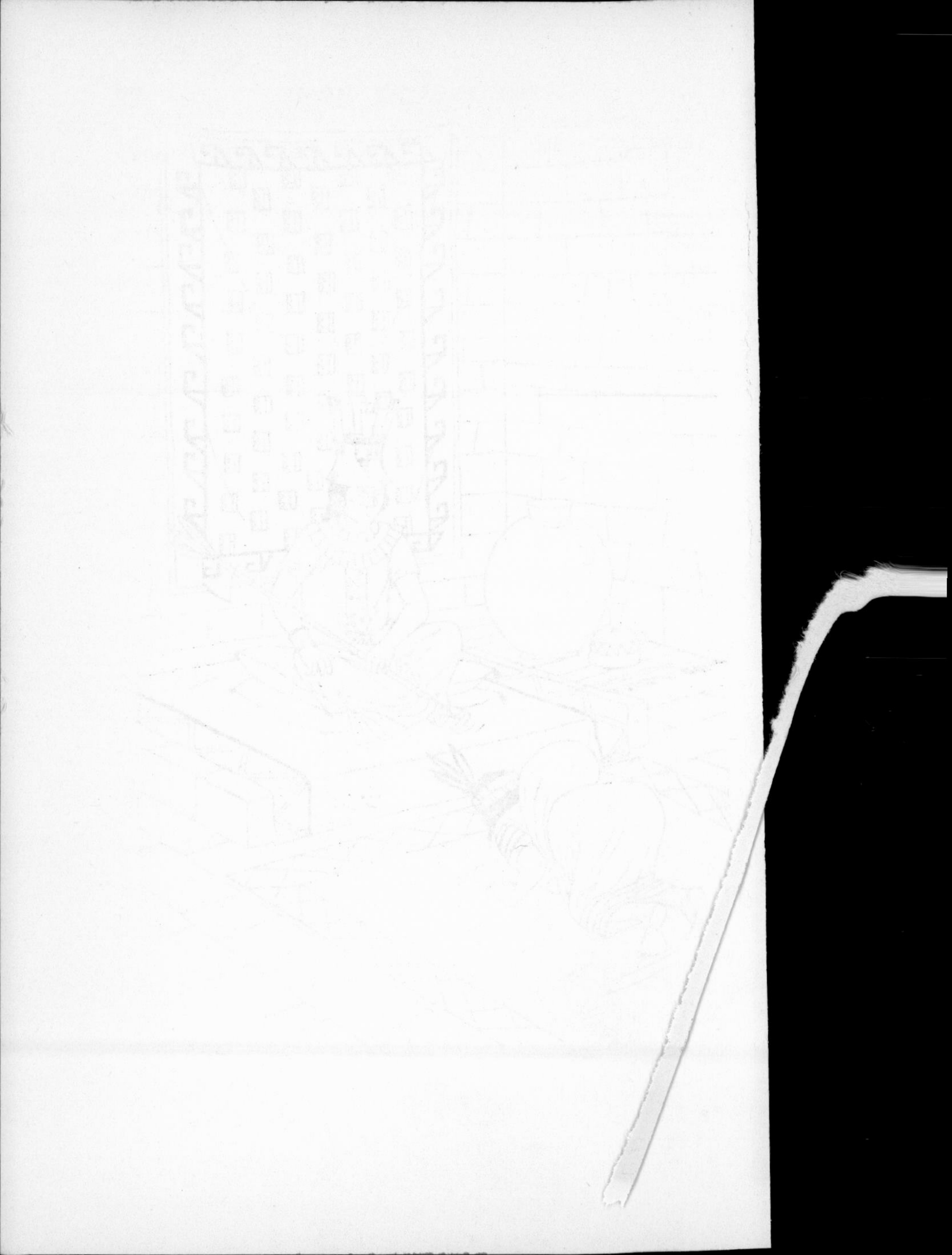

same garments twice. After one wearing, the finely woven shirts of vicuña wool, the feathered capes and kilts, and breechcloths were taken to a storeroom. They too were burned on festive days, as an offering to the Sun.

This was what the common people believed. It may be that the garments were worn more than once, but it was good for people who had so little extra food and clothing to talk of their emperor's extravagances. It gave them the satisfaction and pride of abundance. Certainly no one was envious of the emperor. One is not envious of a god.

4

GROWING UP

Among all classes of Inca society, children were very much wanted. When a woman gave birth to a child, whether she was a farmer's wife, a noblewoman, or even an empress, she was helped by a midwife. Women preferred the help of a midwife who had had twins, because twins were considered a sign of a god's favor.

During the delivery the husband remained at home. He in no way assisted the midwife, but he fasted and prayed. The moment the baby was born, the mother bathed it and herself. An Inca woman was not pampered. In a short while she was up and about, doing her household chores.

When the baby was four days old it was placed on a low cradleboard. The cradleboard stood on the floor, supported on four short legs. Two hoops were fixed to the cradleboard—one at the head and one at the foot. The mother put a shawl on the cradleboard, and then she placed her baby upon it, tied the baby to the board with a strip of cloth, and threw another shawl over the hoops of the cradle. Thus the baby was kept warm without being in danger of suffocating.

The baby, strapped to its cradleboard, went everywhere with its mother. When the baby cried

she nursed it. A noblewoman also nursed her baby, but she had a servant carry the baby for her when she went to visit a neighbor.

A child was named a year or two after its birth. The naming day was celebrated by the baby's family and relatives. Relatives brought gifts, and the child's oldest uncle cut its hair and nails and offered them to the Sun with a prayer that the child should be healthy and enjoy a long life. Dancing and refreshments followed.

The name chosen was a "baby name," and the child shed it when he or she reached maturity. A boy might then be named for his father, or his grandfather, or for certain qualities his parents admired. There were no fixed rules for naming. He might be called Sinhi, which means strong, or Tito, which means generous, or Kosi, which means happy, or he might be named Puma, Hawk, or Jaguar. Girls were named Star, Pure, Gold, and even Coca. The common people were satisfied with a single name, but the nobility and the royal family liked double names. Some had three names.

In the villages young children played under their mother's watchful eye. Little boys had toy bows and arrows, toy spades, and digging sticks. They whirled tops of clay and wood. Little girls played with dolls made of grass or molded of clay. They "cooked" in tiny clay pots and used toy spoons and bowls. At seven or eight children were expected to help their parents. Boys began to herd the llamas and alpacas; little girls ran errands for their mothers. Between the ages of ten and thirteen a boy began to work with his father in the fields. At about the age of fourteen he was taxed as an adult. At fifteen he had to contribute his share of labor to the village *mita*. By helping and imitating their parents, the children of farmers and craftsmen learned all the skills they needed for life as adults.

The education of the children of the Inca nobility was different—it took place outside the home.

At about the age of ten, some of the girls of the nobility were selected for service to the Temple. These girls were called Chosen Women, and they were placed in one of the temples of the four provinces of the Inca Empire. They were taught to weave, cook, care for a house, and make *chicha*—a beer made of fermented corn which was the popular drink of the Empire and is still popular in Peru today. It took a girl about four years to learn these skills. Some of the Chosen Women became the wives of nobles and warriors. Others, however, were dedicated to the service of the Temple. These women never married. They took care of the priests, wove clothing for them and rugs for the ceremonies, and prepared food for the festivals. Some went to live in the emperor's palace, where they prepared his food and wove his clothing.

A few of these girls were designated for eventual sacrifice to the Sun. All the girls were deeply religious and considered themselves especially fortunate in being sacrificed. They looked forward to a happy life in the heavens.

When a girl reached maturity, there was a ceremony to introduce her into womanhood. During the ceremony the girl remained shut up in her home. She fasted for three days—eating nothing at all for the first two days and chewing only a few kernels of corn on the third. On the fourth day her mother bathed her, and washed, combed, and braided her long hair. The girl put on a new dress, a shawl, and white woolen sandals, and a feast was held for her. She waited on the relatives who had come to the feast, and her most important uncle gave her a permanent name.

Boys of the Inca nobility were carefully educated. Schooling for boys began at about the age of twelve. As the Empire expanded, the government needed more and more men to fill jobs as generals, priests, philosophers, and poets. Thousands of administrators, such as governors and *curacas*, were also needed. To insure that they would be available, the Inca had special schools for boys of the nobility, which prepared them for these roles. The Inca even adopted into the nobility some of the conquered sons of chieftains and educated these boys to become administrators.

Late in the thirteenth century, Sinchi Roca founded a national university at Cuzco to educate the sons of the nobles and of the emperor. The men who taught at the university were philosophers, amautas, and poets (*haravec-cunas*), who had learned all the wisdom and lore of the Inca. Since the Inca had no written records, the teachers spoke and the students listened. The Inca believed that memory lay in the heart. Older men always said to the young, "Store the words we speak in your heart." The students were told the myths and legends and history of the Inca. They memorized what they heard as we memorize poems. In fact, the Inca myths and legends were recited in poetic form, with repetitions which made memorizing easier.

Here, for example, is a morning prayer.

> The earth
> Is covered with light
> In order to praise
> Viracocha, the Creator.

The lord of the stars,
Our Father the Sun,
Spreads his hair
At Viracocha's feet.

The mighty torrent
With its song
Is singing the praises
Of Viracocha, the Creator.

So, too, my heart
At every dawn
Gives praise to thee, Viracocha,
My Father, my Creator.

Boys' schooling continued for four years, one of which was spent learning to interpret quipus (key′poos)—the Inca's counting and recording system. A quipu consisted of a main cord which was about a yard long, from which hung smaller knotted strings of various colors. The color of each string and its position on the main cord had a special significance.

Although we have many quipus in museums and

have seen herders today using them in Peru, we are not too sure exactly how the Inca used them. It is believed that the zero was known to the Inca and that a decimal system was used in quipu records. A zero was represented by a string without knots. Other strings had knots representing the units of the decimal system—tens, hundreds, etc. With this system the Inca administrators were able to record the number of families in a village, the number of people in a village, and the number of villages in a particular district. The strings were specially knotted on the spot by a recorder. Other strings showed the number of man-hours of work a village was expected to give to the government. It is also likely that a family's animals and its corn and grain were counted in knots, and records kept of what part it owed to the government collector. Hundreds of such quipus enabled the central Inca government at Cuzco to add up the amount of food that would be harvested and the amount that would be ready for its storehouses.

Quipus were very important to the Inca government, and each kind of quipu had its special interpreter. When a boy had finished his special training and became a quipu interpreter (*quipu-kamayoq* in Quechua), he could look at the strings and recite sums, historical events, and even poetry. Exceptionally proficient boys became quipu re-

corders and spent many years mastering the records of the entire kingdom.

Boys of all classes had an initiation ceremony at about the age of fourteen. Unlike the girls' ceremonies, which were individual, the ceremony for boys was a collective one. In the village a ceremony was held once a year. The mothers of the boys to be initiated wove breechcloths for them. At the initiation ceremony each boy received a man's name, put on the breechcloth his mother had made, and joined the men of the village at a simple feast.

The initiation ceremony for boys of the nobility was more complicated. First the boys, accompanied by their fathers and uncles, had to get permission to hold the ceremony. They made two trips to Huanacauri, a hilltop near Cuzco, which was a huaca—a sacred place.

On the first trip each boy drove a llama from home to be sacrificed in honor of the huaca. Priests drew a line on the boy's face with the blood of his sacrificed llama and gave him a sling, the traditional weapon of the Inca. After sacrificing the llama, the boy returned home, where he received a breechcloth and new clothing. His relatives beat his legs to make him strong and brave, and his family prepared a feast. There was dancing and rejoicing and much *chicha* drinking.

On the second visit to Huanacauri, a week before their initiation ceremony, the boys held foot races. After the races, a boy's uncle gave him his weapons—a shield, a sling, and a club. His other relatives gave him presents too. Now that he had attained manhood, the boy's ears were pierced and a pair of earplugs forced into them to expand the ear lobes. After the initiation ceremony the boys returned to school to continue their studies.

At the age of sixteen, after his four years of schooling, a boy was ready to graduate. But in order to graduate he had to pass some very stiff physical examinations. Even the sons of the emperor had to pass them. The examinations took thirty days and included wrestling, boxing, running, and fighting sham battles on a field outside of Cuzco. Although the weapons the boys used were blunt, they fought so hard and with such zest and zeal that they sometimes fatally wounded their opponents.

The graduating class also fasted for several days. The boys slept on a hard floor in cold barracks with little or no covering. During this time their trainers beat them with clubs to test their ability to endure pain. A young man who withstood all these hardships had, indeed, reached manhood and was worthy of being an Inca nobleman.

The graduation ceremony was a dazzling affair. On that day the young men were dressed as befitted noblemen. Each received a pair of larger earplugs. As a man grew older and his rank increased, he had his ear lobes stretched for ever larger ear plugs. The emperor's gold earplugs were so large and heavy that they rested on his shoulders.

After graduation the young men were assigned government jobs and got married.

Among the villagers, as well as among the nobility, the Inca supervised marriages. The common people were not permitted to marry blood relations. The royal family, however, permitted marriages between sisters and brothers, in order to keep the royal blood within the family. The Inca did not allow the ordinary Indian to have more than one wife, nor was divorce permitted. Even an Inca nobleman, who could have several wives, could not separate from his first wife. He could, however, divorce his second, third, or fourth wife.

Once a year, the village governors lined up the young men who wanted to get married and placed behind each man the girl whom his parents had selected for him. It must not be assumed, however, that the young couples had nothing to say about the selection. There were many courtship songs in Inca folklore, and courtship went on among all young people. A young man watched for a girl he liked and talked to her at the spring or the irrigation canal when she was getting water. Sometimes he met her at a friend's house or at a festival. These meetings were held in secret, however, because it would hurt the girl's reputation if the village gossips knew that she was seeing and favoring a particular young man.

A young man usually asked his parents to speak for him to the parents of the girl of his choice. When two sets of parents selected the same girl, the governor made the final decision as to which boy should marry the girl. He did this after listening carefully to the parents of both boys and the parents of the girl.

After the public betrothal, families paired off to arrange wedding feasts for their sons and daughters. First the groom and his parents went to the bride's home to meet her family. Among the high-ranking nobility, they were carried to the bride's home in litters. When the groom arrived, he knelt before his bride and put a sandal on her right foot. This signified that he was ready to serve her.

The families then turned back to the groom's house, where the bride presented him with a metal pin for his cape and a fine wool shirt and headband she had woven. The groom put on the new shirt and headband and sat down next to his bride to listen to instructions on marital behavior. The teachers were either relatives or a wise man who had been especially invited for this purpose. In the meantime, the groom's mother and the other women present helped prepare the marriage feast. When the talk was finished, everyone ate, and then they drank *chicha.* People always ate first and drank afterwards. No one drank anything, not even water, while eating.

After the feast the bride went to live with the groom's people in a new home which the groom and his relatives had built. The new couple planned to raise their children just as they themselves had been raised, and to pass on to the next generation the traditions and customs of their people.

5

FARMING

The small Indian villages of pre-Inca times had developed many communal activities. Men helped one another build a house, clear a new field, set up an irrigation system, and work the land. This co-operative arrangement was very flexible. A man might help his neighbor make adobe brick and, in return, the neighbor's son or wife would give the man help when he needed it. If the neighbor had extra produce, a man was glad to accept it as payment for the days of work owed to him. Each man also owed a certain amount of work to the community.

These communal activities continued into Inca times, with several obligations added. The *mita* which each man had to give to the community was now extended to cover work on Temple fields and the emperor's fields, work on the roads, and work in the mines. From the age of fifteen to fifty, men had to participate in the *mita*, and no one could escape this obligation. The Inca, however, wisely calculated the amount of *mita* to be imposed on a man. The overseers saw to it that a man still had enough time to attend to his own fields and care for his family.

Most of the people of the Inca Empire earned their livelihood from the land. The fields of the Empire were divided to meet the needs of the people, the Temple, the *curacas*, and the emperor. Each man and his family worked four fields, in addition to their work for the community. When plowing time came and the village overseer announced that the men should go to the fields, they first worked on the fields that belonged to widows, to sick people, and to the wives of soldiers. Soldiers went away to war knowing that their fields would be cared for and their families well fed and clothed. Usually, when men came to help a neighbor, it was customary for the neighbor's wife to feed them. But when working for the widows, the sick, and the soldiers' wives, the men did not expect to be fed.

After finishing this work, the men worked their own fields. They worked next on the Temple fields, then on the *curaca's* fields, and lastly on the emperor's fields. When working for the emperor, the men and women dressed in their best clothing and chanted songs in praise of the Inca.

The order in which the fields were worked was fixed by custom. It is recorded among the Inca that a *curaca* once asked the Indians to break the custom and work his fields first instead. When the higher-ups heard of this, they hanged the *curaca* and his entire family.

Land under the Inca was carefully divided among village families. Each spring the village overseers redivided the land to take care of the marriages, births, and deaths that took place. Each young couple received a piece of land of a size sufficient to support them. Each baby, too, received an allotment.

Land was measured in topos. A married couple received one topo, and a baby received half a topo. In measuring land, a topo was about eight tenths of an acre. In measuring distances, however, a topo was about four and a half miles—some say the distance from one *tampu* to another on the Inca Highway.

The Inca had other measures too. A large gourd was the standard measure for distributing grain to the people. Still other measures were in body units. The distance between the tip of the thumb to the tip of the forefinger was five to six inches. The distance from the tip of the little finger to the tip of the thumb was about eight inches. A man's height, which was about sixty-four inches, was the largest measure, and half of this was another standard of measurement.

The time of day was told by the position of the

sun—dawn, noon, sunset. Units of time were measured by the time it took to boil potatoes. At those high altitudes it takes about an hour to bring potatoes to a boil. When a person said, "I will be there in two boilings," he meant in two hours.

Without irrigation it would have been impossible to farm the land along the coast and in the highlands. Farming in the Andean regions has been going on for over 3000 years, and the Indians had dug irrigation ditches long before the Inca. Under the Inca, streams were redirected to make more room for fields and to enable the fields to get the most water. With their engineering ability, the Inca added many miles of canals, aqueducts, and causeways, which carried water to the steepest fields. They put a steady water supply into Cuzco and even had running water in the Temple of the Sun and in the emperor's palaces. They also built several stone baths with running water. Archeologists today marvel at the engineering of the irrigation canals. Some of them seem to be winding uphill, and yet they worked perfectly.

A farmer was responsible for keeping in good repair the ditch that ran through his own fields, and watchmen stayed up through the night to make sure the irrigation canals were working properly. The amount of available water was carefully divided among villages, so each village received its fair share. In turn, each farmer received his share of water from the village chief. The Indians regarded the irrigation system as huaca. When they moved the stone slabs that acted as gates to let water into the ditches, they prayed to the water and thanked it.

Work in the fields was hard. Despite their skills, the Andeans never developed better farming tools to ease their daily labor. To break the soil an Indian used a digging stick, a three-foot-long pole with a sharpened point that was usually reinforced with bronze or stone. The handle across the top of the pole had a downward curve, and each pole had a footrest on which a man pressed, as we do a spade, to break the soil. A wife worked behind her husband in the field. As he dug, she broke the sod

by means of a heavy stone attached to a short pole.

For fertilizer the people used llama and alpaca manure. Those who could get it also used guano for fertilizer. These bird droppings had accumulated on the offshore islands for hundreds of years. The Inca forbade anyone to visit the islands during the breeding season, in order to protect the guanayes, cormorants, and other fish-eating birds which were responsible for these rich guano deposits.

To sow corn, beans, squash, or potatoes, a man scooped the soil with a spade—a broad, flat stone attached to a pole. His wife followed him, dropping the seeds into the ground, covering them, and stamping down the earth with her foot. As they worked they sang songs to honor the earth, the sun, and the rain.

> Great Sun, mighty Father,
> Watch the sowing.
> May it prosper.
> In the belly of mother earth
> May it germinate,
> May it grow.

In the valleys the Indians planted corn, or maize. It is believed that the maize which the early settlers found in North America had spread there from its home in Central America. It was a very important contribution to the food of the world. In a cave in Mexico, archeologists recently found corn pollen in layers of earth that were estimated to be some 25,000 years old. This indicates that Andean farming dates back pretty far, but how far, exactly, we still have to find out through further studies.

The other main crops in the valleys were beans, pumpkins, sweet potatoes, tomatoes, peanuts, and manioc. The potatoes we call Irish potatoes came from Chile. The Indians called them *papas*. There were also other potato-like crops, such as *oca*. The potato is very important to the highland people, because it grows high up in the Andes. The highlanders worked out a way of preserving potatoes, as they did meat. When the potato crop was harvested, the women cut the potatoes into slices. They alternately dried and froze the slices by leaving them in the sun during the day and in the cold at night. This process turned the potatoes black. They would have seemed unappetizing to us, who are accustomed to eating white potatoes, but they made a very filling, sweet, and easily cooked food for the highlanders.

On the eastern slopes of the Cordilleras the Inca cultivated the coca plant. Among the many legends about the origin of this plant is the story told by a group of Indians who call themselves the Aymara.

Once the Aymara men wandered across the mountains to the tropical rain forests. Accustomed to the meager and coarse vegetation of the highlands, the Aymara were much impressed by the fertile soil and luxurious vegetation of the valleys. But they could find no clear place for starting a field, and so they decided to clear a piece of land by setting fire to it.

Soon the men had a large area of the forest floor smoldering. The fire spread, and the flames rose higher and higher. The smoke reached up the mountaintops to the dwelling of the Snow God. It polluted the clear mountain air, and the Snow God had difficulty breathing. In anger he ordered Thunder and Lightning to hurl rain and hail over the forest to extinguish the blaze.

At the first sound of Thunder the Aymara, knowing they had offended the Snow God, hid in a cave. When the storm subsided and the men came out of the cave, they found that all the lush vegetation had been destroyed. The starved Aymara searched for food. After many days they came upon a shrub with bright-green leaves. It was a coca plant—the only vegetation that had survived the storm. The men eagerly plucked a few leaves and began to chew them. Miraculously, their hunger and fatigue left them, and they were no longer cold. They plucked the rest of the leaves, dried them carefully, and took them back to their villages. From that time on coca has been regarded as a sacred plant.

Because the leaves of the coca plant contain cocaine, the Peruvian highlanders have found that if they chewed coca they were less bothered by cold, by the strain of a day's work, and by pain and hunger. From morning to night, since ancient times, each man has kept a wad of chewed coca leaves in his cheek, replacing it from time to time with fresh leaves, which he carries in a small pouch.

These tiny pouches (*chuspas*), which were especially made for carrying a man's daily supply of coca leaves, have been found in Indian burials that antedate the Inca. Some believe, however, that during the days of the Inca Empire coca leaves were chewed only during feasts and on ceremonial occasions. It is known that the Inca sprinkled coca leaves in their temples as an offering to the earth goddess, Pachamama, to insure an abundant harvest. A half dozen leaves piled neatly in front of a burial place were a humble offering to the dead and to the spirits. When a village chief made an offering for his village, he sometimes used as many as 144 coca leaves, which he neatly arranged in 12 rows of 12 leaves each. At home, Inca women used coca as medication. They brewed coca leaves for stomach-aches and put leaves over wounds to soothe the pain.

Today the coca-chewing habit is necessary to

supplement the meager diet of the Peruvians. A villager consumes about 1500 calories of food daily—half the amount of calories we consume—and coca helps him bear this food deficiency.

Although the Indian population is now less than

half of what it was in Inca times, a third of the Peruvian people are impoverished, despite machinery and aid from the outside. This is a sad change from the days of the Inca, when the Empire's soil supported over eight million people, and everyone was fed, clothed, and sheltered.

In those days the Andeans believed that it was a privilege to work the earth, and every bit of land, no matter how steep, was irrigated and crops grown on it. They thought that the soil, the mountains, the trees, and the grasses were living things like themselves, and like themselves, each had a soul. To neglect the soil, to fail to use it, was like leaving a soul to die, and this was against the Inca religion. It was a man's duty, they said, to improve the soil constantly, to make things grow from it, not to overgraze it, and not to destroy its vegetation. Because of these beliefs the Inca were the best conservationists the Americas ever had.

When no more land was available in an area, and when no more could be acquired through terracing and irrigation, several villagers got together and moved to a new place, forming a new ayllu. If the first harvest was insufficient, the new ayllu received extra grain and potatoes from the government storehouses. If they did not have enough wool for clothing, the government issued them wool, too. With this help the villagers were soon able to fend for themselves. They worked their new fields with pride, and as they worked they sang songs praising not only the gods but their own strength and toil, which helped the soil to yield abundant harvests.

6

THE CRAFTS OF THE EMPIRE

Under the Inca most silversmiths, goldsmiths, stonemasons, and potters lived and worked in the towns. Their products were used by the government and by the nobility. For their work they received food from the government warehouses and regular allotments of wool for clothes. In a way, they were favored above the farmers, because they did not have to pay taxes. The craftsman, like the farmer, was happy to be working at his job and tried to excel at it. He taught his children his craft and his skills.

The metals mined in the Inca Empire were

gold, silver, and copper, as well as some tin, lead, and platinum. These metals came from open-pit mines or were washed out from mountain streams. Miners were drafted from neighboring villages and towns. They prayed to the mines, which they considered huaca, to give up their metals. The Inca permitted miners to work only four months of the year—the warm months. When the four-months' period was over, the miners returned to their homes.

The important metals were copper and tin. Tin mixed with copper made bronze, and out of bronze craftsmen fashioned fine, durable tools, knives, and balls for the ends of bolas. The Indian herders used bolas as men in the North American West use lassos.

Inca craftsmen knew many of the methods for treating metals that are known to us today. They knew how to make the cutting edges of bronze knives, axes, and chisels hard, durable, and sharp. Metals that required smelting were worked in clay furnaces. Instead of forcing a strong draft into the furnace with a bellows, the craftsmen blew into the copper tubes that led to the furnace. In some locations, where strong winds prevailed, they constructed the furnaces facing the winds, so that they would help to fan the flames.

Pure gold was hammered into sheets. Working this soft metal with a bone tool, on an anvil lined with leather, the craftsmen embossed designs on the sheet and cut it to the desired shape. The design might be a man's face, a bird, or a serpent. Craftsmen also used the *repoussé* method we use today—they placed a mold under the gold sheet and hammered the design from the mold onto the sheet. The edges of two gold sheets were folded and clinched together skillfully. Sometimes the edges were heated and welded together; sometimes solder was used. The solder was a copper powder mixed with gum.

Craftsmen also used molds for casting metal. Sometimes they made rough casts and finished the product, after it had cooled, by cutting and hammering. They also made fine castings by filling a specially designed clay mold with wax. The mold was heated, and as the wax melted, it was replaced by the molten metal, which the craftsmen poured into the mold through an opening.

Hundreds of craftsmen were busy turning out gold and silver dishes, cups, and goblets, often inlaid with shells and precious stones, and spoons with straight handles that were highly decorated with hammered designs. They molded figurines of women, alpacas, and llamas, which the nobility used as ornaments and as decorations for their sumptuous litters. The earplugs worn by the nobility and the specially designed gold ornaments which were woven into the royal headdresses were also produced by these craftsmen.

Even with the annual sacrifices of quantities of gold and silver ornaments to the Sun, the Empire still possessed an ample supply, and the craftsmen kept turning out more and more year after year.

Pottery making was also a highly developed art under the Inca. For several thousands of years the people of the Andes had been making things of clay, and by the time the Inca conquered them there were many skilled potters scattered throughout the land.

Among the Andeans both men and women worked as potters. Although the women were skillful and turned out fine water jars and attractively decorated *chicha* jugs and storage pots, the men were the superior potters, because under the Inca they could devote all their time to their craft.

Clays for making pottery were everywhere in the Andes. There were some fine clay beds around Cuzco. Each group of potters knew the potentials of their clay and worked out the best way to temper it to make good pottery. Some potters added finely ground sand, shells, and even potsherds (fragments of broken earthen pots) to make the clay more plastic and durable.

Pottery ranged from the simple, rounded cooking pots, ladles, and spindle whorls that housewives made to the highly decorated, enormous storage jars made by skilled craftsmen. There were jars of all sizes and shapes. The potters also made bowls, plates, goblets, and pitchers. There were pitchers with legs, for balancing on flat surfaces, and pitchers without legs, which could be placed on the ground in scooped-out holes or on a stove.

The simplest way of making a small, round-bottomed pot, after the clay had been mixed and kneaded, was to take a lump of it and shape it with the hands, let it dry for a day or two, and then fire it. Sometimes a potter rolled the clay into long coils and built up a pot with the coils, round and round, until he had the size he wanted. Next he smoothed the sides of the pot with dampened hands, let it dry, then polished it with a smooth pebble and let it dry some more. To achieve a thinner finish, he sometimes pressed the freshly made pot against a smooth stone held inside the pot. The Andeans did not have the potter's wheel, but they often placed a pot on a rounded, specially molded plate and twirled it.

Before the pots were fired they were decorated with red, white, and black geometric designs,

some of which were so well made that they looked like woodwork or metalwork. Some villages had favorite designs, which were used with slight variations, and a pot belonging to a certain region was easily recognized. The designs were simple, yet strikingly strong and pleasing.

Before a pot was painted, it was covered with liquid potter's clay, which was called a slip. The potter rubbed in the slip and let it dry. It filled whatever pores remained in the clay. When the paint was applied with a fine reed brush, it spread evenly over the smooth surface. Experienced potters knew just how long to fire a pot or bowl, how close to the flame it should be placed, and how hot the flame had to be for the desired effect.

Another great Inca craft was their stonework. We still do not know exactly how the stonemasons produced such fine articles with their simple tools. Craftsmen made axes, war-club heads, clod crushers, mortars, and pestles for everyday use. They made round and square ceremonial dishes of stone, with designs in relief, and they made bone and shell spoons, needles, picks, spindle whorls, flutes, and beads.

The best of the Andean stonemasons were drafted to build temples and the emperor's palaces. Hundreds of men worked together on these buildings; and enormous boulders were moved up and down mountainsides, cut to the proper size, and, without plaster, fitted together so expertly that even today a knife blade cannot be pushed between the joints of some of the old walls still standing in Peru.

The Inca, like some of our modern architects,

liked their buildings to be entirely functional. Their magnificent stone constructions are still marveled at today. The walls of the buildings were so beautiful that the Inca left them undecorated. But inside the temples was some of the finest work of the Empire: gold and silver plates; images of Viracocha, the Sun, and other deities; figures of people; and hammered serpents, pumas, and llamas.

Despite the destruction of so much of this work by the Spanish, some of it survived and has been preserved in museums the world over. We are very grateful to the Inca for this rich heritage. When we see a goblet, a gold figurine, a feathered cape or blanket, a war club, or even a simple cooking pot and bowl, the men and women who created them come alive in our minds and hearts.

7

BELIEFS AND CEREMONIES

Religion and ritual were present in all the activities of the Andean people. They worshiped many deities and sacred places. They believed in good and evil spirits. And they saw omens in many things—a rainbow, a falling star, the shape of a cloud, or the hooting of an owl.

Viracocha, the Inca believed, was the creator of the Sun, the Moon, and the stars. The Sun—the life-giver—was the most important servant of Viracocha. He watched over the maturing crops, and he was the father of the Inca emperor. His image, hammered in gold, was a human face surrounded by rays—the Sun's flowing hair.

The Moon was a woman, the wife of the Sun. The Inca believed that the eclipse of the Moon was caused by a great serpent or mountain lion trying to devour her. To frighten the serpent off the Moon, the Indians pointed their weapons at it and shouted.

All the constellations had duties assigned to them by Viracocha. The Pleiades watched over the seeds in the fields, and the constellation Lyra, which looked like a llama, watched over the herds.

Thunder, the god of weather, was another important deity. Like Viracocha he was pictured as a man with a war club in one hand and a sling in the other. Thunder and lightning came from his sling, and from the Milky Way he drew the rain.

The Earth Mother was worshiped too, especially by the farmers. Mother Sea was worshiped by the fishermen.

According to Inca beliefs, the good people

went up to heaven after death and lived with the Sun. There they had ample food, *chicha*, and warmth. Men and women who were not good in life, such as witches, went to live inside the earth. It was cold and dark there, and they were given stones to eat instead of corn. The nobility, however, always went to live with the Sun after death, regardless of what they had done on earth.

When a man died, his wife and other female relatives cut their hair and kept their heads covered with shawls during the long period of mourning. Outside the home, while the body was being prepared for burial, mourners—men and women—moved in a slow dance. The body was placed in a sitting position on a mat inside a cave or in a shelter built of rocks. The knees were drawn up to the chest, and the body was wrapped in layers of cloth. Some of the dead person's belongings were burned, and the rest were buried with him.

When a nobleman died, his funeral rites lasted longer than a farmer's, because some of his wives and servants were killed, to accompany him and serve him in heaven. For a time after the burial the family visited the grave with offerings of food, drink, and clothing to help the departed on his journey heavenward.

After the death of a wife a nobleman was not permitted to take another wife for a year. A farmer was not permitted to remarry for two years. In a farmer's household, where everyone was so dependent on the woman for weaving, mending, and cooking, as well as helping in the fields, it was, indeed, a hardship to be without a wife. A man's brothers and the members of his ayllu tried to help him and his children as best they could until the man could remarry.

In addition to worshiping the deities, the Inca worshiped the numerous huacas—sacred places—which were everywhere throughout the Inca Empire. Mountaintops were huacas, because man could not penetrate them. The emperor's palace, with all his goods, was sealed after his death and became a huaca. Battlefields, caves, springs, quarries, and even the roots of trees were huacas.

There always seemed to be room for more huacas in the religion of the Andeans. When the Inca conquered a village and introduced new huacas, the villagers gladly accepted them.

A man would sprinkle a few coca leaves as he passed a huaca. If he had no coca leaves, he placed a stone near it, as many had done before him. Thus huacas were distinguished by piles of stone. If he had nothing at all to offer, he pulled a few hairs from his eyebrows and lashes and blew them toward the shrine. Many huacas had shelters nearby. A priest lived in the shelter, caring for the shrine and cultivating a small field beside it in honor of the huaca.

The Inca also believed in the existence of evil spirits and supernatural beings. Evil spirits were feared but not worshiped. Some of these spirits, it was thought, had been witches in life, and in death they went abroad at night and did harm. Everyone avoided them. The supernatural beings, however, were friends of man and full of kindness. They punished transgressors with bad luck but never inflicted severe physical suffering.

The Inca nobles, the generals, and the emperor consulted the supernaturals before setting out on a journey. There were several famous supernaturals, or oracles, which the Inca consulted. The most powerful oracle lived at Pachacamac on the Pacific coast, south of what is now the town of Lima. Another, Apo-rimac, lived on the Apurimac River near Cuzco and gave the river its name. This oracle was a tree trunk. The Inca built a house around it and dressed the trunk in women's clothing, decorated with gold pendants and fine sashes. The oracle did not speak directly to the person who came for advice. It made a special noise, a nodding or a shaking of the leaves, and its reply was interpreted by a priest.

There were sorcerers, too, who foretold the future. Some sorcerers drank themselves into unconsciousness with special concoctions they had prepared. When they recovered they told what they had dreamed and foreseen.

Fire was also used to foretell events. This divination by fire was a most impressive ceremony. The people of Huaro, near Cuzco, who were fire diviners, were highly respected and feared. Even the emperor fasted for three days to attend one of their fire-divining sessions.

At the ceremony a diviner placed two ceramic burners, or braziers, opposite each other. As he fed chips into the fires of the braziers, his assistants, hidden behind a wall, kept the flames under control by blowing into long copper tubes connected to the braziers. The fire diviner, weeping and chanting, invoked the spirits of living and dead people to come to his aid. Food and drink were placed on the floor near the fire, as offerings to them. The diviner questioned the spirits and, through ventriloquism, voiced their replies. In the meantime the assistants blew on the fires in the braziers, and the flames leaped high with each reply. This meant that a new spirit had appeared.

There were many other ways of foretelling the future. A priest might sacrifice a llama and study its markings to determine what the outcome of a battle would be. For less important questions a priest sacrificed and examined the lungs of a guinea pig, or even a bird. A man might scoop up a handful of pebbles and count them to see whether his plans would succeed or fail. If the number of pebbles was even, he would succeed; otherwise he would fail. Some men sought omens for the future in a wad of coca leaves. They spat the coca juice onto the palms of their hands. If the juice ran evenly down two extended fingers, the outcome of the plan would be favorable. If the juice ran down unevenly, it was a bad sign.

Among the Inca there was good magic and evil magic. Men who practiced evil magic were hated and feared, and if a man accused of sorcery proved to be guilty, he and his family were killed. To bring sickness or death to an enemy the sorcerer made an image of him and spit on it or burned it. This, the sorcerer hoped, would harm the enemy or kill him. A sorcerer could plant a foreign object in a person's body, the Inca believed, and he could turn a person's insides upside down.

Disease could be cured only by magic and by prayer, since it was caused by sorcery. The plants used in curing were numerous, and today many of them have been found to possess healing properties. The Indians, however, did not know about chemicals. They thought the plants had the magic with which to cure an illness.

A curer had to be a diviner. By praying he divined where the sickness lay and then proceeded to cure it by taking it out of the patient's body. Curing power sometimes came to a person who had been ill and recovered from the illness. To others the curing power came in a dream or a vision. Often, before treating a patient, a curer made a sacrifice to honor his vision and thus gain its co-operation.

With much practice many of the curers were able to diagnose an illness, and oftentimes they used the right herbs to cure it. Some even treated broken bones by putting them in casts, and some sawed off broken arms and legs and did it so skillfully that the patient survived. Skulls were incised while the patient was drunk with *chicha*, and some of these patients survived.

Curers also used hypnosis. It is told that a special room was cleaned and sprinkled with corn flour. The sick person was brought into the room, hypnotized, his body cut open, and the object that was causing the pain removed. The curers were paid with gold, silver, clothing, ornaments, and gifts of produce.

Occasionally, after a diviner had declared a disease incurable, a man attempted to cure himself by sacrificing his own child. This was the most precious offering a father could make. Since the god wanted a human life, perhaps he would take the child and spare the man, on whose support the rest of the family depended.

The Inca believed that when the emperor became ill, his sickness was due to the people's sin. The Inca prayed and confessed and purified themselves, so their emperor would get well.

Priests and priestesses listened to confessions of carelessness in saying prayers, neglect of festivals, witchcraft, poisoning, and even murder. To hide anything during a confession was regarded as a sin. After confession the penitent fasted and bathed in a running stream to purify himself.

The emperor and his household did not have to confess to any priests. They confessed directly to the Sun and asked the Sun to speak for them to Viracocha. After such a confession, they bathed in a river, so the water would carry away their sins.

Men and women prayed both silently and aloud. The common people did not memorize prayers, as the priests and some of the nobles did. The ceremonial prayers of the priests and the nobles were word perfect. Each person spoke directly to the gods with the same respect and careful choice of words he would use in speaking to an older and wiser person. Feasting, drinking *chicha*, and dancing usually followed each ceremony.

Inca ceremonies followed the Inca calendar. The seasons of the year were very important to the Inca, because they lived off the land. Their calendar was divided into twelve lunar months, named for important agricultural and religious events. Since the seasons south of the equator are reversed, the January of the Inca calendar was the equivalent of June in North America. The calendar year began with December, which is like May in the north.

Here is a brief account of the outstanding national ceremonies and festivals. There were many, many local festivals too. People who could not get to a big town or to the capital for a celebration observed the holiday at the nearest huaca. It goes without saying that whoever could get to Cuzco did so for the joy and satisfaction a religious people have in attending important ceremonies.

December, *Kapac Raymi*, was the month of the Magnificent Festival. During this month the Inca held initiation ceremonies for the sons of the nobility. January, *Kamay*, was the month of the Small Ripening. February, *Hatun Poky*, was the month of the Great Ripening. March, *Pakar Waray*, was the month of the Flowers and Earth Ripening.

In April, *Auriwa*, the month of the Dance of the Young Maize, a white llama, brushed and groomed and covered with fine cloths and gold ornaments, was paraded in the plaza before a large gathering. The Inca, like many other Indian groups, had a myth about a Great Flood which had almost wiped out mankind and all living creatures from the earth. A white llama had survived this flood, and the llamas that paraded in the plaza each year were descendants of this first llama.

In May, *Aymuray*, festivals were held all over the Empire to celebrate the month of the Harvest.

June, *Inti Raymi*, was the month of the Festival of the Sun—the most important Inca ceremony. The people believed that the Sun was holding the celebration and that the nobility were his guests at the festival. The emperor himself presided over this ceremony, and every nobleman, dressed in his best and displaying all the ornaments he possessed, came to Cuzco for it.

Professional clowns entertained the gathering and made the people laugh. They wore masks and carried musical instruments—drums, rattles, bells, trumpets, whistles, and flutes. These musical instruments were made of wood, bone, reeds, shell, and metal. The clowns pranced about, pulling in people from the audience to dance with them. Some of the dances were dignified, however. To the sound of a great drum, which a servant carried on his back (the drummer was usually a woman), men and women formed a single line and joined hands. In their bright shirts, dresses, and headdresses they moved slowly across the plaza—two steps forward, one step back. Sometimes the men formed one line and the women another, and danced together with great dignity from one end of the plaza to the other. The emperor, of course, did not dance. He sat on a low gold seat high up on the stone steps of the Temple of the Sun, and looked down on his people below.

The Festival of the Sun lasted for nine days. At dawn on the fourth day, all the Inca came out into the great plaza in front of the Temple, stretched their arms in front of their faces, and made kissing noises as a greeting to the Sun. Llamas and alpacas were sacrificed, and then the emperor stood up, holding two golden goblets filled with *chicha.* The goblet in his right hand he offered to the Sun, his father. The emperor poured it into a gold jar which was connected by tubes to the Temple. The *chicha* flowed through the tubes into the Temple, giving the impression that the Sun was drinking it.

From the goblet in his left hand the emperor took a sip of the *chicha* and then handed the goblet down for the nobles to sip and pass around among themselves. This royal gesture of friendship, of drinking with his noblemen as equals, meant a great deal to every nobleman present. Not for another year would any of them share a drink with their emperor.

The emperor, the priests, and others of royal blood now entered the Temple to offer gifts of silver and gold to the Sun. People of lesser rank brought gifts too, but they were not permitted to enter the Temple of the Sun. After walking up its two hundred steps, they remained outside, and the priests carried in their offerings.

Next there were more sacrifices of black llamas and alpacas, and then a priest cut open the first animal and examined its heart and lungs. If these proved healthy and unmarred, and if the lungs were still full of air, everything in the Kingdom of the Sun would be successful. If the animal was unhealthy, the people knew that there was misfortune ahead, for somehow they had displeased the Sun.

July, *Chawa Warkis*, was the month of Earth Purification. During this month priests made sacrifices to the huaca which presided over the irrigation system of the Cuzco valley, and similar festivals were held to honor the huacas at the irrigation canals all over the Empire. August, *Yapa-*

kis, was the month of Everyone's Purification. Sacrifices, brought to Cuzco from the four provinces of the Empire, honored Water, Frost, the Air, and the Sun. September, *Koya Raymi*, was a dry month, and the Queen's Festival honored the change in weather. In October, *Uma Raymi*, the Inca held the Festival of the Water. The people prayed for rain, because the crops that had been sown in August and September would fail without it.

In November, *Ayamarka Raymi*, there was the Festival of the Dead. During this festival people made offerings to their dead ancestors. It is possible that this worship of ancestors was based on a fear of the dead. The Inca may have believed that unless they treated the shades of the dead with respect, the shades might molest the living.

In addition to these monthly ceremonies there were many others, which were held on special occasions, such as drought, an earthquake, or a war. During these ceremonies everyone who was not of noble rank had to leave Cuzco. Men and boys marched in procession through the streets, wearing red shirts with long fringes and ornaments, great feathered headdresses, and shell necklaces. They carried small dried green birds and white drums. At these ceremonies the only sound was the sound of the drums; the people were silent.

Human sacrifices were offered only on these solemn occasions, or at the coronation of a new emperor. It is said that at one emperor's coronation two hundred children were sacrificed—boys of ten and girls between ten and fifteen. The children were feasted before the ritual, so they would not appear hungry before Viracocha.

After two days of fasting the special ceremony ended. There was feasting and dancing and people were gay again, confident that Viracocha, through the intervention of the Sun, would grant them their prayers.

8

THE LAST OF THE INCA

In 1532 the Spanish conquest of Peru began, and the power of the Inca Empire came to an end. The conquest of Peru was accomplished by Francisco Pizarro, a fifty-six-year-old soldier of fortune, and his small group of adventurers. They had been around Panama for some three years and had begun making sorties southward in the Pacific until they had reached and passed the equator. There a pilot in charge of Pizarro's boat sighted a large balsa with a sail and succeeded in capturing it. The Indians aboard were Peruvian noblemen. The Spaniards marveled at their fine wool clothes and, especially, at their silver and gold ornaments. Pizarro had already found gold ornaments along the coast, and the Indians, who were quite friendly and unafraid, said that in their country there was a great supply of these shiny metals.

In 1529 Pizarro visited Tumbes. The people there were friendly too, and the Indians accompanied him back to Panama. Pizarro now rushed to Spain with samples of the gold he had found. He was granted permission by the Spanish Crown to conquer the lands to the south, and in 1532 he landed in Tumbes again. Fortune, he discovered, was playing into his hands. A civil war between Atahuallpa and Huascar—the rulers of the Inca—had split the people and weakened the great Empire.

Atahuallpa, victor of the civil war and now sole ruler of the Inca, had no fear of Francisco Pizarro, with his 180 men and a few "short-necked llamas." He continued bathing in the hot sulfur springs of Cajamarca, knowing that it would take the Spaniards many, many days to reach him. His 30,000 trained soldiers were camped around the palace, enjoying a rest after the civil war, but the emperor was confident that they could be quickly alerted and moved into action. Having behind him the experiences of three centuries of Inca conquest, Atahuallpa calmly awaited the arrival of the bearded strangers.

In the typical fashion of the conquistadores, the Spaniards looted, burned, and destroyed the peaceful villages in their path as they moved inland from Tumbes to Cajamarca. Finally the first contingent of Spaniards—forty men, led by Hernando de Soto—arrived at Cajamarca.

When the Spaniards invited Atahuallpa to inspect their camp, he readily accepted. Dressed in his beautiful robes, with a colorful feathered mantle, a gold and silver headdress, gold sandals, and ornaments of precious metals, Atahuallpa was carried in his gold and jeweled litter into Hernando de Soto's camp on the evening of November 16, 1532. As the Inca procession entered the camp, a friar ran up to the litter. Through an interpreter, the friar asked the Inca to declare his allegiance to the Spanish king and the white man's God. Alarmed and suspicious, Atahuallpa stiffened and replied with Inca pride that he was the son of God himself. He could not pray to another god.

To the simple friar this statement was heresy. For anyone but Christ to declare that he was the son of God was unthinkable. At a total loss as to what to do next, the friar thrust a Bible into the hands of Atahuallpa. This was an age of miracles, and perhaps the friar hoped that the Bible would make the Inca realize the true faith. Atahuallpa had never seen a book, nor had he ever accepted anything from hands other than those of a royal Inca. Therefore, he did not take hold of the Bible, and it fell to the ground.

To the Spanish soldiers with their simple Christian faith, letting the Bible, the holy book, fall to the ground was the greatest sacrilege. Had the gold image of the Inca god, the Sun, fallen to the ground, the Inca Indians would have been just as dismayed. De Soto seized this opportunity to order his soldiers to surround the astonished Atahuallpa.

If the proud Inca had commanded his soldiers to fight, he might never have been made prisoner, since his retinue far outnumbered the forty Spanish soldiers. But Atahuallpa remained silent. Used to obedience, his soldiers did not even protest. They let their emperor be carried into De Soto's camp and locked up in one of the rooms.

The Spanish now demanded that Atahuallpa pay them a ransom in gold and silver for his freedom. Atahuallpa promised to fill the room in which he was imprisoned—it was twenty-two feet long and seventeen feet wide—once with gold and twice with silver. At his order, swift *chasquis* set out over the entire length and breadth of the Empire to bring in the gold and silver. Headdresses, arm bands, earplugs, nosepieces, sandals, breastplates, dishes, and spoons were hastily collected from the temples and the homes of the nobles, packed on the backs of men and llamas, and sent to Cajamarca. With amazing speed, the ransom began to arrive and fill the prison room.

Although the Spaniards were fearful that the Inca would organize an army against them, there was no revolt. The people were accustomed to obeying the orders of their *curacas*, the *curacas* looked for orders still higher up, and at the very top, the administrators awaited the command of the emperor himself. Atahuallpa chose to remain silent.

As soon as the ransom was paid, Pizarro ordered Atahuallpa strangled. Several of the Spaniards urged Pizarro to spare Atahuallpa's life, as he had promised he would, but Pizarro was afraid that the emperor would organize a revolt against him. He ordered the gold and silver to be melted down into bullion, and this, plus some gold and silver that was later obtained at Cuzco, came to a total of about twenty million dollars. Only a fifth of this money went to the Spanish Crown. Pizarro kept the rest and divided it among his brothers and his men.

It is believed that much more gold and silver was en route to Cajamarca. But when the carriers heard that Atahuallpa had been murdered, they turned back and hid their loads in mountain strongholds. This treasure was lost to the Spaniards, and no amount of torture they inflicted upon the Indians helped them to find it again.

After killing Atahuallpa, the Spanish, with their captives and camp followers, moved on to Cuzco. They now traveled in greater comfort than they had when they crossed the Andes from Tumbes to Cajamarca. Along the route, whenever a *tampu* and its storage buildings looked promising, they stopped and looted it. They made the villagers along the Inca Highway carry the loot on their backs to Cuzco. In the villages they seized the corn and potatoes that the farmers needed in order to survive until the next harvest. When the farmers protested, the soldiers burned their homes.

At Cuzco, the looting and destruction of property continued. The Spanish tried to collect all the gold and silver of the Empire at once. Keepers of buildings, who tried to prevent the soldiers from taking away sacred images, were beaten. When soldiers thought that a keeper was hiding some valuables, he was tortured until he confessed or died. The proud Inca nobles were thrown out of their homes, and their palaces and wives were taken by Spanish soldiers. The great llama herds that belonged to the emperor and to the Temple were killed off wastefully.

The atrocities of the Spanish conquest jolted the Inca out of their blind obedience to authority. To prevent the people from revolting, and to give the impression of keeping things within the law, Pizarro placed Manco, a younger brother of Huascar, on the throne. Pizarro told the people of Cuzco that he had killed Atahuallpa because Atahuallpa had murdered Huascar. For a while Manco remained the Inca figurehead. The people were again confused as to what action to take and so did nothing but submit.

As time went on, the Peruvian villages were joined together in enormous estates and given away by the Spanish Crown as rewards to the men who helped conquer Peru. These estates were called encomiendas, from the Spanish word *encomendar*, meaning *to entrust.* Supposedly the Indians were entrusted to the Spanish landlords to be taught Christianity, but actually the Indians were "entrusted" into slavery.

The Spanish conquerors took advantage of the existing Inca customs which suited their plans for exploitation. One of these was the custom of the *mita.* When Pizarro felt the need for a good port on the Pacific coast, he used the *mita* to recruit hundreds of men for the building of it. With the help of Inca craftsmen and engineers he laid plans for a large city, which eventually became the city of Lima, capital of Peru. The city was an imitation of some of the finer Spanish seaports, with palaces, gardens, and plazas.

Entire families were drafted under the *mita* to mine gold and silver. Soon there were thousands of men in the mines. They had to work for thirty-six hours at a time, using only a simple crowbar to loosen the ore. Then some fifty pounds of ore were wrapped in a sack, tied around a man's middle, and slowly and painfully carried up a flimsy ladder. Three miners at a time carried their bundles upward, lighting the way with a taper attached to the thumb of one of the men.

Under the Inca, men worked only four months a year in the mines, and then they returned home. Under Spanish rule men were supposed to work only four months too, but the working arrangements contained so many other provisions that most men never returned to their home villages again. One of these provisions was that a miner could not leave the mine until he paid his debts. If a man died, his children inherited his debts and had to work them off at the mine.

It was almost impossible for the Indians to avoid going into debt. Until the Spanish conquest the Indians had used no money, but the Spanish introduced money and paid the miners in reals and pesos. A man earned the equivalent of about fifty cents a day, or even less, and after he had eaten everything brought from home, including his llamas, he had to buy food in stores controlled by the Spanish management. Everything was very costly at these stores, and often the men were talked into buying things they had no use for. Thus they went hopelessly into debt, and were forced to work on and on at the mines.

In addition to the *mita*, every male had to pay taxes to the Spanish in money and produce. The taxes for men from fifteen to sixty were fixed at eight pesos a year. Five pesos had to be paid in cash, three in produce. The Indian farmers had no money, and to earn the money to meet their cash obligations, they worked the land of an encomienda. The pay for this work was even lower than that in the mines.

On the encomiendas the Spanish introduced new crops: wheat, rice, barley, rye, alfalfa, and a broad bean that thrived at high altitudes. They brought in poultry, sheep, goats, pigs, horses, donkeys, and mules. They also brought in grape-vines, olive trees, and sugar cane. The Spanish crops were worth more on the market than the corn and potatoes the Indians grew, so the Indians began to grow wheat wherever possible in order to pay their taxes with this produce. But they continued eating their old native foods.

When the Indians left their own fields to work for an encomendero—the holder of an encomienda—their fields suffered. A man's neighbors were as badly off as he was, and so they could not help him out. The fields worked for so many centuries with love and joy suffered from the neglect. The irrigation system began breaking down, because much of the water was diverted to irrigate the encomendero's fields and pastures. There was neither the time nor the man power to mend the irrigation ditches and watch over them.

The new towns that were growing up were not built on the poorest land, as in the days of the Inca. They were built on rich bottom land, originally reserved for growing food. Indians were pushed off their fields to make room for expanding towns and church lands. As the cattle industry developed, the Spanish cattlemen drove the Indians off their fields to make more room for pasture.

Soon a new class of landless people sprang up. Homeless, they wandered along the roads, seeking a day's work here, a week's work at another encomienda. When they were hungry, the men stole food.

Another class of people was growing up too—the children of the marriages between Spanish men and Indian women. Most of this new generation became townspeople, tradesmen, and artisans—not farmers.

Poverty and diseases (many of which were brought in by the Spaniards) began to take their toll of the Inca. By 1561, less than thirty years after the Spanish conquest, the population of between eight and sixteen million had dwindled to only a million and a half. This was not an age when anyone the world over coddled a conquered people, but the atrocities of the Spanish conquest shocked even some of the Spanish conquerors.

In 1535 a Spanish friar by the name of Bartolomé de Las Casas—who was about 300 years ahead of his times—began to fight for the rights of the Indians.

Las Casas was sixty-three years old then, but he was so indignant at the treatment the natives of Central and South America were getting from the Spanish conquerors that he secured passage back to Spain to talk to the king. A pamphlet he wrote, "The Destruction of the Indies," was translated into several languages and aroused public sentiment for the Indians all over Europe. Lawmakers in Spain helped Las Casas by drafting new laws for the Indians, which the king finally signed.

Briefly, these new laws provided that no Indian could ever, no matter what the circumstances, be made a slave. If an encomendero died without leaving an heir, the Indians on that encomienda became royal wards. Indians were not to carry burdens for the Spanish—there were horses and mules for that purpose. Indians were to have self-government in their own villages, though they could not leave their villages without permission, and they could not bear arms or own horses. No Indian was permitted to sign a contract and be liable for it. (Too often an Indian put his mark on a document, such as a contract to work in the mines, that he could not read, and he and his sons were then held responsible for fulfilling it.) Indians were to be paid wages for their work on the encomiendas but were not permitted to ask for excessive pay. Liquor, which was not good for the Indians, was not to be sold to them.

These new laws looked pretty good on paper, considering the times. But when Las Casas returned with them, he found there was no way of enforcing them. The Spanish officials of Central and South America would not co-operate. And so the Peruvians remained an impoverished, undernourished people, without hope or joy, and with only bitter hatred for their conquerors.

Early in 1536 the Inca emperor, Manco, having succeeded in organizing an army and escaping from Cuzco, led 200,000 men against the Spanish. Under cover of darkness the Inca soldiers, who knew the terrain well, crept up and surrounded Cuzco. At dawn cries and the blowing of trumpets awakened the Spanish. The Inca army had only primitive weapons—slings with burning tufts of wool, rockets with lighted sulfur matches, and burning balls of cloth filled with gunpowder—but they worked. Within one day Cuzco was a shambles.

Inside the city, Indians built stone barriers to keep the Spanish cavalry from charging out of Cuzco. But the wily Pizarro managed to escape with about 240 men. They entrenched themselves within the fortress of Sacsahuamán, where they remained for a whole year.

The Manco revolt sparked small-scale rebellions throughout the Inca Empire. Groups of Indians fell upon encomiendas, burned houses, and massacred the encomenderos and their families. A few encomenderos were permitted to live in return for working as armorers for the rebels. The Indians began to use Spanish weapons and horses.

Desperate, Francisco Pizarro dispatched men by boat to plead for help from the Spanish governors in the Caribbean countries. In return, he said, he would share Peru with them. Help came from Pizarro's right-hand man, Diego de Almagro, who returned from Chile and, in April of 1537, put the army of Manco to flight. Manco did not lose hope, however. He continued guerrilla warfare all over the Empire.

The Spanish soon became involved in a civil war between the forces of Almagro and Pizarro. They fought for several years, during which Almagro, Pizarro, and his brother were killed. Since Manco was still fighting guerrilla warfare, his younger brother Pallu was declared emperor by the Spanish. But he was literally a palace prisoner and could do nothing for his people.

After the death of Manco, two of his sons succeeded him and continued their guerrilla warfare against the Spanish. Indians from all over joined up, and hundreds left the encomiendas, preferring starvation to slavery. But in 1571, Tupac Amaru, Manco's second son, who was now emperor and head of the guerrillas, was captured. A rope was put around his neck and he was led to the great plaza of Cuzco where once, in the Temple of the Sun, the Inca emperors had been honored. There Tupac Amaru, the last of the Inca emperors, was beheaded.

A throng of Indians watched this execution in mournful silence and listened to the last words of their emperor, who called upon their righteous god to witness the enemies of the Inca shedding his sacred blood.

The Spanish left Tupac Amaru's head on a pole in the great plaza. Day after day, as soon as the gates to Cuzco had opened, crowds of Indians entered and squatted in silent prayer before the head of their emperor. After a while the Spanish authorities grew afraid that the Indians might be planning rebellion. They took Tupac Amaru's head off the pole and buried it with his body.

For the next two centuries after the Spanish conquest, despite great progress made the world over, there was very little improvement in the

CUZCO

lot of the Peruvian Indians. When Peru became a free country in 1821, the revolution held no meaning for its large Indian population. Even today, in both Peru and Bolivia, enormous tracts of land lie wasted. Indians are living below subsistence level, and they are still leaving the land because of economic pressures. Although the old ayllus have been re-established in many villages, the majority of Indian farmers today work on large estates.

But every oppressed people has a legend of a savior who will come to rescue them, and there is such a legend in Peru. Among the peaks in mountain hide-outs and in hidden valleys, the Indians say, there are men waiting for the right time to strike and reinstate an Inca emperor. These men have kept the Inca language and religion pure. Wise men go among them, teaching their children the wisdom of the ancients. Although on the surface these men are humble llama and alpaca herders and potato farmers, they have hidden gold treasures, which the Indians hope will one day be seen in their proper place—in the emperor's palace and in the Temple of the Sun.

On that day, it is hoped, an Inca will sit again on the golden throne of the Empire of the Sun.

INDEX

INDEX

* Indicates illustrations

Recommended Books About the Inca

Handbook of South American Indians. (V. 2, The Andean Civilizations; V. 5, The Comparative Ethnology of South American Indians.) Edited by Julian H. Steward and published as Bulletin 143 by the Smithsonian Institution, Bureau of American Ethnology, Washington, D. C., 1947.

Indians of the Andes, Aymaras and Quechuas, by Harold Osborne, Harvard University Press, Cambridge, Mass., 1952.

Recommended Books About the Incas

Handbook of South American Indians, (Vol. 2, The Andean Civilizations; Vol. 5, The Comparative Ethnology of South American Indians.) Edited by Julian H. Steward and published as Bulletin 143 by the Smithsonian Institution: Bureau of American Ethnology, Washington, D. C., 1946.

Indians of the Andes, Aymaras and Quechuas. Harold Osborne, Harvard University Press, Cambridge, Mass., 1952.